a dark boat

a dark boat

poems by
patrick friesen

Copyright © 2012 by Patrick Friesen

Anvil Press Publishers Inc.
P.O. Box 3008, Main Post Office
Vancouver, B.C. V6B 3X5 Canada
www.anvilpress.com

All rights reserved. No part of this book may be reproduced by any means without the prior written permission of the publisher, with the exception of brief passages in reviews. Any request for photocopying or other reprographic copying of any part of this book must be directed in writing to ACCESS: The Canadian Copyright Licensing Agency, One Yonge Street, Suite 800, Toronto, Ontario, Canada, M5E 1E5.

Library and Archives Canada Cataloguing in Publication

Friesen, Patrick, 1946-
    A dark boat / Patrick Friesen.

Poems.
ISBN 978-1-897535-91-2

  I. Title.

PS8561.R496D37 2012   C811'.54   C2012-901158-4

Printed and bound in Canada
Book design by Marijke Friesen
Interior photographs by Patrick Friesen

Represented in Canada by the Literary Press Group
Distributed by the University of Toronto Press

The publisher gratefully acknowledges the financial assistance of the Canada Council for the Arts, the Canada Book Fund, and the Province of British Columbia through the B.C. Arts Council and the Book Publishing Tax Credit.

CONTENTS

a dark boat 11
the song outlives all 12
rua azul 13
rua da saudade 15
the clarinet's brilliant dream 16
black horse square 18
dark cathedral 19
widow 20
sombra 22
blind in the summoner's arms 23
danza gitana 1 24
danza gitana 2 25
the sun shines through the cracks of the
    shithouse door 26
waiting 28
a day like this 29
lorca 31
grand piano 32
dark night of the tree 34
that wheel of fish and lilies 37
lurching through a funeral 39
the trumpet's last hanging note 41
almost 60 outside peña de la platería 42
both sides of the door 44
ava gardner 46

a crow glides into black silence   47
night   48
her solitude soiled with shadows   50
unclothed   51
tulips   52
balcony   53
green dress   54
blue marsh   56
shabby suit   58
where something blooms   59
burned-out house   61
telling time by the dog among the tulips   62
among these things   64
yellow light falling on the road   66
the wildness no one has haltered   68
it was five in the shade of the afternoon   69
many believers other than the dove   70
cemetery   71
lament blesses the road   72
palma del río   73
moving on up   74
the end of things   76
somersaults   78
dove   79
estrella   80
sol y sombra   81
open grave   82

each day holds its little deaths for a while   84
white town   85
hung out on the dancer's tree   86
barrio santa cruz   89
this woman in sunlight is the one you love   90
keeping it a voice away   91
diver   92
pillars 1   93
pillars 2   94
the dead march slowly   95
walking on a missing bridge   97
anna   100
cornada   101
shoes sink into the river   102
exile   103
the bull in moonlight   104
silence   105
out of one silence after another   106
and then the rain falls   108
alluvial   109
goya   111
goya's playground   112
palmas   113
hora   114

glossary   116
acknowledgements   119

Puertas, puertas, y puertas. Y más puertas.

("Muy Lejos" by Blas de Otero)

A DARK BOAT

you are alone
and you mean precisely that

half-lit by the lamp
you have nothing

on the wall a poster
of a fadista you once heard

long-legged in her longing
waitress in a three-table café

so far to go from
a nursing mother to death

the world is quiet outside
though you know it's writhing

you can't speak
about the world

the fadista sang
of a dark boat

you make do
with the night you have

THE SONG OUTLIVES ALL

walking through a life
the heart flickers out of step for a moment
a voice breaking through
a singer bereft of childhood
a nostalgia for what may not have been
the cradle and the shawl
or nostalgia for the end

the story is slight and best sung
the song outlives all
you can almost hear it at night
in some tired bar
carpenters have not yet built

the singer is never the same
and the carpenters are dead
longing is made from this
and from imagined love

the singer has one foot on a chair
as she sings through the smoke
no one is drunk though
they are not themselves
and it is always easter tomorrow

RUA AZUL

the jostle of her passing
and you look back over your shoulder
catching her dark hair and
the whorl of red and yellow on her stockings

crossing liberdade you find your way
up the steps to bairro alto
still thinking of the graffiti
on a woman's slender legs

bending streets and the luso
with its fado posters
a satanic cat infesting a doorstep
turns to gaze at your dying shoes

you snap an elusive photograph
which you'll never develop
this is nothing like the woman
walking down rua azul

you heard those footsteps before
but nothing ever happened then
and where were you when
the only street ran through you?

you could be on your knees
crossing yourself
there's so much architecture
in the lonely gestures

in the words you've heard
and sung and said fragments
of conversations and taxis
foundering in the night

RUA DA SAUDADE

who you are
the one who glances
passing by

I don't know
where this street goes
like many others
it changes names

bending through
shade and light
going nowhere and
arriving

three women stand
in an open doorway
a dog barking
from some courtyard

jittery I turn around
in this place where
someone turned around
before

you know what I mean?
walking as if I'll get there

THE CLARINET'S BRILLIANT DREAM

saints and mary gliding
through narrow streets
a dark-haired boy
slowly marching
behind the band
his eyes wide and
shining

sobbing when
the band disperses
the night coming down
and his mother's hand
calming him into
the clarinet's brilliant
dream

marching around
the church
down a roman road
marching through
grass and flowers and
beneath the sparrow's
wings

marching with
light feet and
blowing eerie
sounds through
the broken branch
in his little
hands

and the clarinet
dreams the boy
on the road no
one has walked
dreams him toward
the band's silver
encore

BLACK HORSE SQUARE

more ash than fire more
trouble than loneliness and
the sailor always drunk

in heat the unrelenting
drone of cicadas wraps
the milky way around

them like a room and
they resign themselves to
a jealousy of absence that

song sung through smoke
shawls and drownings off
the cape of no good hope

the singer outside her door
shaving her legs
beneath the washline

DARK CATHEDRAL

how can he not be a widower
in the dark cathedral?

he enters from a cold fall sun
into the charred columns of christ

burned out long ago to slag
a sullen mourning without grief

he wants to crawl out
down the bairro alto stairs

he wants the gloomy thugs
without a prayer

he wants a sluttish voice
from the balcony

WIDOW

she has loved death
the widow at the window
has lain with it
you don't know what's behind her
in the dark room
what she will enter when she turns
for a moment a breeze blows
the curtain before her
you think she has vanished
but her hands lie on the sill
white and gaunt
and she has hated death

no one knocks at her door
she will not answer

SOMBRA

your shadow burning on horno de oro
beside a window of song
blurred hand at the guitar's strings
a slashing rhythm that could draw blood

what if the demon got out
does it? yes some nights it does
sniffing for red raw wounds
the room possessed

in the doorway they couple
her legs around his waist
hooves clattering
in the street

and it's all a theft
holy christ it burns
your northern shadow
reaching out its arms
for the black shawl

BLIND IN THE SUMMONER'S ARMS

he stumbled down the stairs
into the garden of eyes

leaving the stone wall's shade
he slid through a fence and came upon the cedar

a dream of hanging ladders of fire
and fearing the wordless night ahead

he lay down in darkness
blind in the summoner's arms

the garden filled with swollen leaves
of tongues of words

a long unknown night
and no one there but him

leaving his shoes behind
barefoot as an orphan

DANZA GITANA I

a rib cage beside the road
sun bleeding into grass

a shawl wrapped around her waist
she raises the hem of her skirt with her left hand
her right arching above her head

eyes downcast
the eyes of blackbirds

what's hidden
beneath children's eyelids

silver water
willows and

dream

DANZA GITANA 2

your eyes follow the slow curve of her spine
down her long back to where her dress begins

the languor of her arms her precise hands
the hammering of her heels on the floor

hands clapping on and off the beat
and a raspy voice tearing the veil

wrenching theft from the night of your throat
you reach for darkness in the pockets of your coat

THE SUN SHINES THROUGH THE CRACKS OF THE SHITHOUSE DOOR

a christian in mecca
on his way to the whores
to get as drunk as it takes

it's his poems the caliph wants
neither the whores nor the cross
are an impediment

as the cynic said
sun shines through the cracks
of the shithouse door

and the beggar throws back
the rich man's coins
demanding his applause

where are the poems now
did he recite them
walking through the garden?

the deputy of god
listening to the eloquence
of the tongue

where are they
these two tall princes
of green paths and water?

wherever they vanished
to the whores or heaven
through the narrow door

wherever they went
the nightingale listened
and flew

WAITING

a clattering of cutlery
inside your head the
breakfast table in shambles and
bees at the hollyhock
a long stalk's shadow
on the white wall's dream

and christ burning
in the civilization of
willow lily and bougainvillea

dying in heat born
in the rain of the world
falling through jerusalem leaves
a tree of nightingales
the bulrushes of the blackbird

dishes can wait
everything can wait

A DAY LIKE THIS

don't visit we're doing our washing
says lorca's neighbour
and it means they're naked
it's monday or perhaps thursday
but it's a day where simple dignity
flutters in the backyard

and a day like this is a knife
lying on a butter dish
with bread crumbs on the table
a day like this is no worse
than another day like this
grasshoppers flitting in the tall grass

no one chooses a day like this
no one claims and
no one lives through
a day like this spins slowly
toward the shadow
of evening's parole

LORCA

heard water in the aqueduct
before dawn in la colonia

and if there had been light
could have seen childhood

water flowing is the shortest time
eternity is a poor word for this

what can be done about a dream
of black veils and a crucifix

what can be done when you've
forgotten your mother's prayer

only death listens to fear
only his body hangs on to him

smelling the road's dust
hearing the rifle's bolt

GRAND PIANO

before
it was before

beneath his grand piano
with angelina and concha
during a barrage

before

before rosales
calle angula
and esperanza

before alonso
calle duquesa
gonzález

before víznar
la colonia
and tripaldi

before the truck
parched air
and the olive grove

lorca

playing his piano
in the alhambra
among the fountains

playing his grand piano
to the ghosts of water
and moorish arms

before
it was before
and still

DARK NIGHT OF THE TREE

the tree
where john lay drunk
with christ the swoon
of that of that love
drunk and yes drunk
among the paths of
a spanish garden

yellow eyes staring feral
from the top of
the stone wall and
a ladder into
night's turret

bare feet damp
with dew the
cedar's scent the
only way toward
what toward what
was john's abysmal
ridiculous
bliss

forgetting himself
and skinned but
the wind but
the cedar leaning
over them

how can you
forget so far how
can you?

only the tree
remains and a few
words lost among
languages the tree
broken
to a man's height
and want

you stand
there in spanish
sun before the tree
a dazed man
in a stupid time
that moment betrayed
again and you
still wanting the
darkness that burns
in the soil of
soil

and wouldn't you
love to wouldn't
you breathe
in the old branches
of the cedar
bellowing like tom waits
in november
calling like flint
for a fire
wouldn't you love

that disease

THAT WHEEL OF FISH AND LILIES

from open windows
they lean over the street
with their craving arms

from the red windows
a hundred tongues call
for blood and honey

everything passes through
your nerves those silver strings
tuning among the irises

flagellant in the fire
your words mangle
within earth's hallucination

and your throat burns
with coals of sound
lungs larynx and uvula

she hangs your skin on a nail
and *holy holy*
in the blasphemous river

she gathers ashes
spreads them on water
that wheel of fish and lilies

a hundred tongues a thousand
clamour in the afternoon's heat
calling for death's incarnation

LURCHING THROUGH A FUNERAL

you smell wet dirt
in the morning shade
along the foundation

the window won't open
enough for the horizon
to slide in across the sill

an old woman's drunk
lurching through a funeral
of a sly river in july

grasshoppers and gophers
in the wheat and dust
a dead car in the slough

and she doesn't belong
no one's seen her before
nor her sky-blue eyes

THE TRUMPET'S LAST HANGING NOTE

he salutes the neighbours
leaning out of their windows
shouting his name
and urging on his ragtag
band of nanny dad
and grandpa the
drum glinting in the sun
like serious metal
and the boy calling
back over his shoulder
for them to march slower

they are exiles of
somewhere each in
their own forgetting
the boy leading them
toward the perfect
exit beyond traffic
and the outdoor café
the beat shifting
to a shuffle and
the trumpet's last
hanging note

ALMOST 60 OUTSIDE PEÑA DE LA PLATERÍA

the alley is as long as anyone's life
it bends like anyone's life
you sit on a cold stoop in the dark
waiting for the song you've waited for
gypsies walk by in black
guitars slung over their shoulders
laughing out of the east like a memory
the moon tilting into the courtyard
drunk with age and ancient youth
and tonight the rain is thirsty
tonight you are finally invisible

tonight the rain is waiting to fall
filled with its longing for earth
a mongrel sidles near and stops
raising its snout to howl
then slowly lowers itself
looking up at you or the moon
you extend your hand
and it eases its weight fully
into the buckled cobblestones
and you don't know your age

you hear the heat
somewhere over the wall
somewhere in that courtyard
the staccato of black shoes
hand claps and a familiar guitar
and yes the rain is thirsty
and the stone gutter waits
for the running water of music
and tonight you will return
to your room on horno de oro
awake to the splattering rain
on the street outside your window
to the rain that falls
on a tile roof on a cedar tree
the rain that falls through you
in your sleep

tomorrow you'll
listen to the darro rippling by
in the shade you'll watch
christ swilling sangria
with a spanish thirst

BOTH SIDES OF THE DOOR

1.

october enters your bed
with the click of the door
slowly you fall back to sleep
in a dream of red leaves
later she tells you she stood
a long moment
on the other side of the door
then walked into the world
to catch a bus

2.

in your dream of budapest
the streets are wet with rain
on a bench your father sits
bent forward in sorrow
you look up to the waiting silhouette
in a fifth floor window
and remove your arm
from his shoulders
to climb the stairs

3.

a weeping at the cemetery
as a young woman is buried
a light breeze along the wall
carrying the scent of lemons
you gazing through the gate
through the rows of ash
to the cemetery wall
where the sailors fell
to earth

AVA GARDNER

shoeless on tobacco road
piedmont dirt between her toes

singing through baptist church
toward an all-night world

long lazy meals
the sun simmering into moon

head back eyes closed
listening to a dj spinning jazz

her laughter raucous as rooks
sly as green eyes at a slant

all that reckless ecstasy in the flesh
then the barefoot walk home

beauty that didn't need a mirror
that careless mirror

just once a helpless glance
from its crazed mercury

A CROW GLIDES INTO BLACK SILENCE

you see them like this
in morning light dragonflies
from nowhere blue-sky
spooks with staring eyes
shaking solar dust
from their wings tilting
and careening in the suddenness
of their born bodies

you standing in place
on home street or rua azul
a place between things
coming or going whatever
the weather the stones
with their dates where
nothing is lost or
remembered

a crow glides into black
silence on the church roof
or onto a branch above
the day's carrion
gazing it to earth and
watching the sailor's
horizon opening a
golden door

NIGHT

a shovel across his shoulder
he walks through yellow fields
toward the stream where
night is buried

cattails burn with blackbirds
their smoke rising into
dusk a drunkard
in the branches of
a willow

the man of men
thrusts the shovel in
with his foot

he is already dead
in the dark mirror
of water

how can you tell
between the hiss
of rain and
flame?

words the ancient
squabbles
man standing
in a squall with his hand
on fire

feet in the raw
dug earth

HER SOLITUDE SOILED WITH SHADOWS

across miles of evening
an iron bell

later a nighthawk drops
and you wait for the whirr
at the bottom of its parabola

something to wonder at

some thing

a ripple of dark
along your arms

a shape sifting along the foundation

the smell of earthen cellars

such a strange
attention

it may be her
leaning against the wall
her solitude soiled with shadows
and if it is
the sky reddening
you can break from
the world

UNCLOTHED

rain among
cypress needles
before day falls

in the white bedroom
you unclothe yourself
and are not human

you turn from the book
toward the appearance
in the mirror

going to ground
on the quick

TULIPS

two tulips bent
like gravity a death
a third defiantly
yellow

the room wants
to leave through
the open door

a widow walks
the hallway
looking for a way
back in

she catches her breath
there is no one to
touch her ever but
the yellow tulip
where she sat
at the sill rain falling
on her hands

BALCONY

the nights you lit light
your brain stuttering
between music and rain
both holding your memory
and maybe the facts
god only knows and
blesses them the way
a still wind unnerves
the leaves

the nights you fumbled
through green jerusalem
somewhere on the rail
nijinsky off-balance or
the great blondin crossing
the watery border
of god and man
the fiery dream
and the falls

the nights abandoned
to abandonment
nothing wild but
absolutely wild like
the young woman
raising her white blouse
to offer her breast
to the one and only
child

GREEN DRESS

it will kill me
kill me

you in bare feet and a green summer dress

there's a long car
around the corner
perhaps a limousine
or a blue cadillac

you in the pale light of your summer dress
so light it flutters when the air stills

your eyes closed
your head with its black hair
tilted back to the sun

it will kill me
whatever it is
this will kill me
what I've carried forever

I don't like long cars
they hold a human
like a little seed
while the driver never talks
there's just too much distance

but you across the yard
naked in your green dress
you

BLUE MARSH

crows rising drag
their feet from earth
trailing soil and roots

the oil of a dead chevrolet
shimmers in the blue marsh
a radio and the red

lips of a dream and
flies gathering around
a spill

lean green impala
sizzling in july with
long spear grass

through floor boards
the dash hot and cracked
by sun flares

and crazy arms skinny
arms spreading wide
all that day

a hundred years and
a knocked over bottle
of spirits

haze rising from a
forgotten slaughter
and birth

black racket of flight
and what in the world's
come over you

SHABBY SUIT

he slouches in a corner of shade
the wind could take him in his shabby suit

there are nooks in the world he has been
windows where he left his eyes behind

in front of a flawed mirror nothing fits anymore
he licks three fingers to flatten fly-away hair

perhaps a fiddle at the door or a mandolin
how does he see his way out?

WHERE SOMETHING BLOOMS

that shadow walking
before you on the sidewalk

goodbye eliot

something
you won't see again

a shadow on reimer avenue
that would be 1959

early wynn

that would be
dr. schwartz
with his crude dentistry

or one slender flint
of brain cell sparking
on a wheel

not a step taken
since *sea of love*
and *broken hearted melody*

your shape burned
into that sidewalk

the brain keeps playing
chemistry with you

and you
just want to find your way
back to the balcony

where something
blooms

BURNED-OUT HOUSE

a knife on the plate
beside the bread
an elbow on the table
a hand and a pair of hands
a hymn sung
a story by memory
of an absent man and
the end of his footsteps
and a fire burns
in this room of secrets
this room of the one
secret of absence
long silence then
the voice again
not praying now
nor singing a hymn
the floor beneath
the table is bare
but for a saucer of
sour milk

TELLING TIME BY THE DOG AMONG THE TULIPS

you have a corner of garden
with montbretia and prairie grass

there are days you tell time
by the gardens in your life

or perhaps by the dog who slept
in a hollow among the tulips

while you are on earth
it is difficult to believe in absence

what you remember is a door
through which you entered

some arriving horizon
a place to set yourself

the limp dog thrown into
the trunk of a '53 dodge

what you have is a chair
beside japanese irises

small animals moving
through tunnels beneath you

you watch their dark faces appear
sniffing the nervous air

what you recall is the ghost
on your father's hands

AMONG THESE THINGS

a shutter swaying in the wind
is the dead singer's voice

you walk clumsily among these things
stones wild grass and wind

the usual things that never surprise
until one day one hour

nothing is counting your life down
but your own wrist

that shadow on the path
walking to town

YELLOW LIGHT FALLING ON THE ROAD

to be shaken by a voice
and taken as a stranger
in your own house

and like your life
the voice disappearing
in the dark

this is not something small
like the time between breaths
this is not time

you follow the night rustle
of water running along the gutter
to the singer's house

like serpents bougainvillea
breathing in the night
above the door

someone moves
across the fragile light
of the window

nothing can be found
in the house
or put together

shutters bang open
yellow light falling
on the road

THE WILDNESS NO ONE HAS HALTERED

your tongue runs foul and your prayers grow simpler
how does a man accommodate everything?
struck in the night by something like a wing or a cloak
the body relinquishes once again its claim

looking over your shoulder you see a dead man
your eyes are the eyes of all the dead and
you wonder at the birdsong you heard long before
your birth and the star bursts lighting the night sky

the weather comes between you and something else
playing you with broken time it opens you up
to what's there the wildness no one has haltered
a horse more spirit than flesh

IT WAS FIVE IN THE SHADE OF THE AFTERNOON

you don't need to know anything
other than *lament for ignacio sánchez mejias*
don't need to know anything beyond
it's all over. rain falls into his mouth

a white mule gazes at your window
you don't know what to do about that
those long white ears and irascibility
the patience of two thousand years

smoke passes before the sun
day following day and night
and everything that once bewildered
bewilders

there's no speaking
there is no heart for it
your lover looks across the room
knowing dark and light

not buddha not jesus did this
though they had their nomad words
still you salute them leaning
in the shade

then it's done and rain
comes to wash away blood
rain arrives in the world's
afternoon at five

MANY BELIEVERS OTHER THAN THE DOVE
for lala isla

there is no way through
lorca's dark eyes
how could words like this come
from one man's tongue?

those sensual lips
were meant for someone
they never found
in moorish waters

lost in havana or las ramblas
caught on the train
between all the cities
of andalucia

there is no reason
for a voice like this
between the processions of the cross
and the bombardment of albaicín

so many blood feuds
so many solitary rifles
a stark hate that had to break
the spanish chalice

and spanish walls must be painted
again and again
until they are red as roses
in full blossom

CEMETERY

rifles leaning against
those useful walls
waiting for dawn
when the next generation is
old enough to shoot
in the headlights of a truck

LAMENT BLESSES THE ROAD

gone to sea and away
cooks and poets lemon
leaves aniseed and sepharad
a sigh along the road the only
sound left of princess merchant
and the deputies of god

chains across the quadalquivir
its golden tower the vanishing
light as ships load and drift
away berber egyptian and jew
turning a last time toward triana
to hear that remaining darkness

lament blesses the road
and the horizon beyond
which are dreams and
the words of exile
the words and seeds
of breath
held back

PALMA DEL RÍO

animal and man and
the appetite of the fat
of the land

bulls blossoming
into poppies walls pocked
with lead the cemetery holds
a landowner's rage

the wet glassy eye
of a cat watches from
behind the tulips

only the tolling bell
only the olive's thirst
live here only the
priest boiling grass

we have always been
hungry he says *we*
have always

his nose running
with snot the boy
will open the shutters
to steal away

MOVING ON UP

exhausted with heat
flung across your bed
you watch the wind
slide through a window
and tear the room
from the building

glancing off trees
off houses and
rising up the mountain
to slash through
the streets of
the pueblo

you get up
to find leaves
a snowstorm and
the honking
fanfare of a
mule

your first thoughts
are not of god
hallucination or
miracle but how
the hell did this
happen

they're all there
waiting at the bar
susie on her cell
marcos and dominique
with her elegant
wrists

paella on the table
sardines in oil red
wine spilling and
the room teetering
on the edge of
plunder

THE END OF THINGS

a sparrow flutters on the sill
listening through the screen
to messiaen singing
about the end of things

sidling with a breeze
fluffing its brown chest
the sparrow's heart pumps
itself to ruby

then twittering for a moment
like a shower of sparks
through a cloudless day
it is gone

SOMERSAULTS

no matter
the sky
with its hair
on fire
all that's left
is staring and
acrobatics grabbing
the hook
hanging there
you turn
somersaults
between earth
and sky

DOVE

the morning wakes in panic
an iron door banging in the wind

a dove calls from the nightmare
of the devil's interval

a cow batters its skull
against a low stone wall

shores succumbing
to oily seas

a white donkey stumbles
through the streets of jerusalem

even the piebald horse has forgotten
the language of the road

our wandering has stopped
as we settle at the foot of the stairs

the dove freezes
on the monument

ESTRELLA

estrella with her black hair up
and the hunger of her glittering eyes
walks the road in her dark stockings

she is the layer out of bodies
the one who groans in ecstasy
when day falls silent as light

she will crawl naked across you
searching for your mouth
with her lavender lips

don't expect the lamb of god
or the swooning tree of buddha
expect nothing at all

estrella will suck you to a husk
in the hours of night
while you sleep with the dead

when you rise
the child will greet you
with a knife

SOL Y SOMBRA

the cool noonday moon
rivets a bare landscape

magdalena of the garden
playing to the light

but her voice calling
from the shade

a line of light slides
along the shine of a street

filtering through the lattice
of a lace house

from a white balcony above
a parrot's blue come-on

while estrella dries her black hair
in the sun

OPEN GRAVE

she raises her skirts at death
spinning to send it away

she hears clicking fingernails
smells sour breath

blood running down her legs
she whirls until her feet turn blue

arms flung out
she leaves the trampled ground

once more escaping
the mouth of the great devouring

but when she leaves the gate behind
she hears the echo of her steps

knows she will dream the people
gathered around her open grave

EACH DAY HOLDS ITS LITTLE DEATHS
FOR A WHILE

out of the dark
a white town appears

nothing disturbs the light
of the mourning dove's fear

the scent of a cigar on the path
a loose page of newspaper

then almost nothing
for almost that long

the town flaring
awake

WHITE TOWN

a white town
on a hill of afternoon light

an old man with a long-handled roller
looks up as he whitewashes a wall

reaching for the sky
and always pulling back

he stops for water
rippling down his throat

he shakes his head
as he awakens

HUNG OUT ON THE DANCER'S TREE

offering her hands
with their long fingers
ana parrilla appears like
red kaffir lilies in the fall

dying

there are agonies in
the face of possession
the derelict face
turning aside

hanging from the sky

her long gestures
bent at the elbows
gathering the night
to herself

loosening

finding her way
down night stairs
away from the glimmer
of lamps

tower and well

earth that makes
sky possible
bolts on the cross
flying away

the lust of prayer

and that dark embrace
where they meet
hung out on the dancer's
tree

BARRIO SANTA CRUZ
for eve joseph

sauntering toward her marriage
in the old jewish quarter alone
and bare shouldered she
moves through centuries of
perished footsteps and ash

moors and jews soleares
from triana drifting across
the river and the barefoot
walk of faith a band
gathering in some street

processions come and go
hooded men staggering beneath
the masks of history
while she carries the dark
accounts

light from a side street
draws her around a bend
toward the street of the fallen
where her marriage waits
in the arms of a thief

THIS WOMAN IN SUNLIGHT IS THE ONE YOU LOVE

gazing from three crosses'
shade across the table
at your bride

half-finished sangria a
spill and green olives lit
like still life

her eyes closed
this woman in sunlight is
taken up

there is nothing else no
theology no history no
thousand year grief

only this returning story
without a past that
unfolds here

where she is away

KEEPING IT A VOICE AWAY

what hangs from the structures?
culture and radiant thought?
what cadavers swing above the squares
the filthy rivers
like the chiming clocks of god?

buttress and arch hold up the sky
keeping it a voice away
all the sad chanting and
gestures of hand and
law

who hangs on the scaffold?
who kneels at the cemetery wall?
and where is the fire
that flamed up the cedar tree?
where is the tree?

sancho kneels at the deathbed
his donkey grazing near the door
brays through the fields
along the streets named
for miracles

the stone bell tower is
a matter of time

DIVER

knife in hand
something to slice
open the water

a boy in the river's tree
groping through weeds
and memory

rising to his wedding day
to light and laughing
one arm raised from the dead

alive he shouts
erupting with strands of hair
clinging to his face

PILLARS I

those who sit on pillars speak with god
or so say saints and certain virgins

you open the shutters before dawn
slow cool night air wisping in

the window is dark and wet as earth
crawling with worms and potato eyes

mules and even the dogs are silent
there is a rank smell of afterbirth

who can believe in saints and virgins
and all the other killers of night?

PILLARS 2

left by pigeons and saints
shit streaks pillars and statues

butterflies too leave excrement
on the iron bells they light on

and you in your pleated pants
where do you live?

THE DEAD MARCH SLOWLY

muffled songs and talk rise
from the sludge of underground
streets as a slender rib
bone works its way up
into the weather that remembers
and forgets and forgets
again

what is turned over
by the spade what
has grown for seven
times ten years is
a garden of skulls
in the great unwashed
city

a woman kneeling in
the square her dress
dark and sodden with
rain has turned her
face from the tower
to hear the heart
pause

when the rain lets up
at dusk and the orange sun
lights up a stone wall
the dead march slowly
through the streets of
the pueblo behind the child
with his drum

WALKING ON A MISSING BRIDGE

toes and heel
absence where
the foot arches

that sculpture
the intention
in its path

or motion the
motion of a bridge
heel to toe

crossing a square
to find
a bench

where a flock
of pigeons descends
suddenly

surrounding
the old woman eating
a sandwich

crumbs scattering
in a half circle
before her

birds flutter
aloft when
she rises

her foot rocking
heel to toe and
lift

walking
on a missing bridge
across the guadalquivir

ANNA

anna looks lost
as she walks through town
with slow long strides

she wears a straw hat
over long hair
with a yellow rose at her wrist

it was a gift she says *from a stranger
something almost romantic
at the bus stop*

there are men who admire beautiful
women they will never touch
they offer a gesture which is more

anna is never lost
whether she walks through king's cross
or moscow metro

where she is
she hears the mourning dove
at 7 a.m.

fingers at her lips
she knows other
languages

CORNADA

gallows fire and belief
impossible questions from
the masters of the lord

in triana the dancer
with her long fingers
calling out grief and exile

a rusty bayonet in the shade
of the river's bank the smell of
decay the bull's flawed eye
and chop and gallito gored
belmonte perfectly still on
his bandy legs

festering in the hills above
granada near the solitary
olive tree near the stars
the white of lorca's bones
shining beneath earth's
cornada

SHOES SINK INTO THE RIVER

master leans against a broken wall
propping it up till dark
shoes sink into the river
where no one walks anymore

boys clambering up the steps
shake water off like dogs
their fathers hammering iron
into birthright

the path is guadalquivir
or flying buttress
whatever holds mind
to flesh

the arch of a footbridge
across the darro
a stone missing in the ceiling
of that aching flight

EXILE

home of the sleeper's dream
that forgotten descent into
limes green olives
the rivers of thirst and
birth

home of exile the
sails and wings of
voyagers slipping into
the muddy clothes of
earth

such a thin membrane
between cross crescent
and spade
such a forgotten
gaping door

THE BULL IN MOONLIGHT

emerging dark from heaven
on the horizon then
passing sudden silver
as a moon again and
again spun in a circle by
a boy in shabby pants

night is filled with harsh
breath the pawing of
bull's hooves where he waits
in profile waiting in his
other world

old death gives him up
for an hour returning to
lascaux or some other
time

a last dark pass
the boy vaulting horns
in a somersault

dawn slides up from the quadalquivir
his hand holding up torn trousers he
gazes on the city's golden ruins
a woman arrives in red shoes
to offer him an orange

SILENCE

shadows on the river's wall still
moving still carrying their loads
through the summer heat

in the narrow streets of
the jewish quarter the shade
of a man dragging a cross

lit by headlights cemetery
walls hold the darkness
of a thousand souls

it is still beneath
the cedar where the visitor
leaves his walking shoes

OUT OF ONE SILENCE AFTER ANOTHER

a cold map of bayonets and
ditches holding the many and

many have stirred to storms
in the mountains thunder and
white skies of the south the
way wind moves among
the red poppies and time
happens

they come crawling out of
one silence after another
they begin with broken nails
to scratch at the earth to dig
through the forgetting through
the small words of the mouth
in the valley

hands grasp at roots or gouge
snow away from the door
legs still trembling from their
running from their standing on
last legs waiting to fall to their knees
to slowly fall sideways falling and
rolling into their graves

this is the astronomy of
death all the stardust
that fell ashes to ashes
that shaped the man
disappearing around a corner
the woman shivering beneath
a thin red sweater

AND THEN THE RAIN FALLS
for irina kudriavchenko

and then the rain falls
after sun and sun and sun

irina says in ukraine
a rainy day is for weddings

don't pity the horse standing
alone in a field of rain

a snake rustles in the eaves
clear water running down the spout

why is this day for weddings
why is no one marrying?

a mule under a branch
not bothering to shake its coat

ALLUVIAL

is this where they don't exist
have not been born? the dead
dancing and clapping black
honey oozing through femoral arteries

is this what we long for
the music of jails?
do we want to hold every
thief in our arms?

they will sing you
into thin air and sing
you down they will
break your shackles

always the songs escape
their cells there is nothing
there to hold in hand

that alluvial moment
morocco sacromonte and
sepharad where songs
hook into each other

songs arrive and leave
owned by no one
only the dead have
the voice to sing them

standing on their own bones
they sweep away the broken
bombs of atocha

the arsonist loves
his room torching it
time and again

GOYA

his hands all over
the black walls of his house
calling the dog crawling
out of the mud

saturn slavering and
bug-eyed devouring
his child in hallucinations
of the darkest god

monstrous night black
and gaping the spittle
of thunderbolt neutrons and
appetite

the town idiot sordid and
sallow hungering for
meat for the son in
his jaw

headless in his grave
goya never rolls over
after the executions and
the cemetery walls

after dark housebound days
there will never again
be anything to roll
him over in his grave

GOYA'S PLAYGROUND

an old man on a swing
kicking his spindly legs
barefoot and grinning at the top
of his flight

PALMAS

an echo through
olive groves brown hills
scattered with poppies

how the world began with
a sharp handclap then
staccato fingers swirling

across strings like
a devil fleeing
through sacromonte

melisma soleares and
the white-sailed ships
drifting home empty

the rhythm the rhythm
is there in the skeletal trees and
hands

handclaps becoming the dark
hands of the gardener
at day's end

HORA
for sebastián flores flores

his back to the sun
burning among rows
he never seeks the shade

bent over with shears
or digging by hand
he slowly relentlessly
finds the weapons

he closes the rift
smacks it flat
with the palm of his hand

rising
he looks at his work
motionless in the face
of the day

filling time
or not that
at all

GLOSSARY

Puertas, puertas, y puertas. Y más puertas.: Doors, doors, and doors. And more doors.
rua azual: blue street
rua da saudade: longing street
sombra: shadow
danza gitano: female Gypsy dancer
palma del rio: town in Spain
sol y sombra: sun and shade
barrio santa cruz: old Jewish quarter in Seville
cornada: wound from the bull's horn
palmas: the percussion of hand-clapping in flamenco
hora: hour
fadista: female singer of Portuguese fado
liberdade: a main street in old section of Lisbon
barrio alto: section of Lisbon
the luso: a theatre in Lisbon where fado is often sung
la colonia: the house, outside Granada, where Lorca was held captive the last night of his life

The following ten names, which appear in the poem "grand piano," are names of people, streets, and a town, Lorca encountered in the days leading up to his execution.

angelina: maid in the Lorca home in Granada
concha: Lorca's sister

rosales: Luis Rosales was a young admirer of Lorca's work. He hid Lorca in his parents' house for several days before the Falangists arrested Lorca

calle angula: street where the Rosales family lived

esperanza: sister to Luis Rosales; she supplied Lorca with daily newspapers while he hid there

alonso: Ramón Alonso was a Falangist who was directly involved in the arrest and execution of Lorca

calle duquesa: a street in Granada where Lorca was held for a night

gonzález: a schoolteacher who was held at la colonia with Lorca, and several others, then executed with him before dawn

víznar: a village just outside Granada on the way to Lorca's execution site

tripaldi: the guard at la colonia who told Lorca that he was not being held to dig fortifications for the Nationalists, as he had been told, but was going to be shot before dawn

peña de la plateria: a club in the Albaicín district of Granada where flamenco is played

horno de oro: a street in Granada

las ramblas: a major street in Barcelona

havana: capitol city of Cuba

andalucia: the southern territory of Spain

albaicín: a district in Granada

guadalquivir: river running through Seville to the Atlantic

sepharad: name of the idea of the Jewish community in Spain until their expulsion some five centuries ago

pueblo: town
paella: popular, seafood-based, dish in Spain
ana parrilla: great Spanish flamenco dancer
soleares: one form of flamenco music
sancho: Don Quixote's companion
triana: traditional Gitano neighbourhood in Seville
sacromonte: traditional Gitano neighbourhood in Granada
gallito: great Spanish torero
belmonte: great Spanish torero
darro: one of two rivers running through Granada
atocha: the largest railway station in Madrid

black horse square: a square in Lisbon on the Tagus River. This was a place where people landed. It had several previous names. After the great earthquake of 1755, it was rebuilt with a large statue of a horse in it. English sailors called it Black Horse Square.

ACKNOWLEDGEMENTS

Thanks to Kwantlen Polytechnic University for financial help with my travels to Lisbon and Granada in 2005.

Thanks to the British Columbia Arts Council for financial help in traveling to Spain in 2010.

Thanks to the Fundácion Valparaiso, especially Pilar Parra and staff.

Thank you to Simon Andrewes for taking me through Granada and into the hills outside Granada, guiding me through Lorca's last days; also, for letting me know where I could find the cedar tree beneath which St. John of the Cross might have written *The Dark Night of the Soul.*

I would also like to acknowledge Lala Isla, Barbara Lamplugh, Andrea Jacobson, Alexandre Kudriavchenko, John McManus, and Anna Gorban for conversations at Valparaiso. Particularly, I would like to thank Lala for ongoing answers and information relating to aspects of Spanish history, literature and music, and for her generous friendship, and to Barbara for opening her home to Eve and I in Granada. Also my appreciation to Dominique Estéve for friendship at the Pavana and in the streets of Mojácar, and to Lourdes at the Miranda in Madrid.

Thanks to P. K. Page for her insistence that since I was going to Lisbon I absolutely had to travel to Granada to see the Alhambra because she'd always wanted to but knew she no longer could.

And, always, gratitude to Eve.

PHOTO BY MARIJKE FRIESEN

ABOUT THE AUTHOR

Patrick Friesen has published more than a dozen books of poetry, most recently *Jumping in the Asylum* (Quattro Books, 2011). He is also the author of a volume of essays and co-translations, with P. K. Brask, of Danish poets Niels Hav, Ulrikka Gernes and Klaus Høeck. Friesen was short-listed for the Governor General's Award for *A Broken Bowl*, received the Manitoba Book Award for *Blasphemer's Wheel*, received the P. K. Page Founders' Award for Poetry (Malahat Review), and has twice been short-listed for the Dorothy Livesay Poetry Prize (BC Book Prizes). Friesen has also written several stage and radio plays, text for dance, and has recorded two CDs of spoken word and improv music with Marilyn Lerner. A former resident of Winnipeg, Friesen now lives on Vancouver Island.